The Five Noble Truths

Affirming Your Brilliance

By Paul Rodney Turner

Editor: Carol D'Costa (www.caroldcosta.com)

© Copyright 2013 Paul Rodney Turner
All rights reserved.

Version Date: Monday, April 22, 2013

Australia

ISBN: 978-0-9850451-3-5

The trademarks, service marks, logos and devices displayed are the exclusive property of the author and are protected under US and various international jurisdictional trademark and copyright laws. Use of any of these instruments without prior express written consent of the author is strictly prohibited.

The design, images, text and overall layout are protected under US and international law as copyrighted materials. Anyone who claims, displays, reproduces, copies or creates derivative works for commercial or non-commercial purposes without prior written consent from the author is in violation of copyright laws and will be held liable for copyright infringement under the relevant jurisdictions.

Dedicated to Tinkie Quinn.

Thank you for being such a magical, soul-affirming, and loving friend in my life.

Introduction 9

Using Affirmations 11

Yantra Meditation 13

I am Powerful 15
- Strength 15
- Potential (kinetic energy) 16
- We are Little Gods 16
- Managing our Mind and our Karma 17
- Aligning with your Core 19
- Practical Namaste 20
- Purest Love 21
- The Soul is Unborn and Undying 22
- Detachment 24
- Dealing with Attachment 26
- *Yantra & Meditation* 28

I AM Protected 31
- Sense of Security 31
- Peace of Mind 32
- Interdependence 33
- The Synergy of all Things 33
- We are Never Alone ... Just Forgetful 35

Yantra & Meditation	38

I am Perfect — 41
- GET IN TOUCH WITH YOUR ESSENCE 41
- LOVE THY SELF 42
- YOU ARE ONE OF A KIND 43
- ACCEPTANCE 44
- DO NOT BE DISTRACTED BY EXTERNAL ILLUSIONS 44
- *Yantra & Meditation* 48

I Am Prasadam — 51
- MERCY 51
- INTERDEPENDENCE 53
- SYMPATHY AND EMPATHY 53
- SELFLESSNESS 54
- BLESSING OTHERS 55
- SERVITUDE 55
- THE GOPIS 56
- *Yantra & Meditation* 58

I Am Prosperous — 61
- THE LAW OF ATTRACTION 61
- YOU DESERVE THE BEST 61
- WE ARE ALL EQUAL 62

THE RAIN DOES NOT DISCRIMINATE	63
WE ARE HEIRS	63
PROSPERITY CONSCIOUSNESS	64
SELF-SATISFACTION	65
Yantra & Meditation	*66*

Concluding Words 69
What is a Yantra? 71
SYMBOLS AND THEIR HIDDEN MEANING 71
AIMS AND OBJECTIVES OF YANTRAS 72
USES OF YANTRA 73
MY PATH TO YANTRAS 73

What is a Soul Yantra? 75

INTRODUCTION

One evening while sitting at the table with pen in hand, I asked myself a simple question: What is special about me?

I allowed my pen to flow without thinking too much about the answers, and to my surprise I came up with five affirmations that coincidently all begin with the letter "P". Easy to remember, and as you'll see they touch upon the very core of our existence. Thus was born what I call *The Five Noble Truths* that now serve to guide me through my life: **I am Powerful; I am Protected; I am Perfect; I am Prasadam; I am Prosperous.**

My hope is that these affirmations will give you the solace, strength, and the wisdom you need to succeed in your life as well.

In expanding on the meaning of each affirmation, I have drawn from the teachings of various esoteric and spiritual traditions. Essentially, I was writing this book for my*self*. As I typed each word, I took on the role of an empathetic friend offering encouragement. I want you to know that everything contained in this book was written with the utmost sincerity by the hand of an encouraging friend.

An affirmation is a declaration of something that is true. My hope is that these affirmations will resonate with you as they have with me and that you will embrace and apply them within the context of your own spiritual tradition.

Our spiritual journey is a very personal one, for no two people truly walk the same path—even those within the same religious community. As the saying goes: you must "fly your own plane," on the path of righteousness. So, *bon voyage!*

I offer these five Noble Truths to you with love.

Paul Rodney Turner

USING AFFIRMATIONS

Affirmations have been an important part of spiritual tradition since the beginning of time. Expressing a positive and heartfelt affirmation to yourself can only serve to strengthen your resolve to be the best you can and to heighten and nourish the expectations of others.

Affirmations come in many forms, including mantra, the written word and in yantras—the ancient art of sacred geometry.

Part of the challenge of incorporating a positive outlook on life is the need to first reprogram the mind to respond in the way that is beneficial to your desired goal. For too long, we have allowed our minds to be polluted by the selfish desires of corporations and their false advertising. As a result, we now find that corporate marketing messages have become an integral part of language and culture. Getting a tissue has become getting a "Kleenex", having lunch has become "going to Maccas"; in other words, the act has become synonymous with corporate branding.

The first step on the path of self-empowerment is to monitor the activities of our wayward minds. Take the time to observe your instinctive responses to information and the experiences that unfold around you and objectively decide if those responses are desirable or not. More than likely, they are not desirable and probably causing you unnecessary anguish and hardship.

When you make the effort to shut down the false programming inside your mind and any negative influences coming from the outside by repeatedly affirming your soul brilliance through affirmations, you will quickly discover just how enslaved you had allowed yourself to become.

I highly recommend you use these Five Noble Truths to affirm your brilliance on a daily basis. You will find that it will be most effective if you do this the first thing in the morning and the last thing you do before sleep. Calm your mind, and then say them with conviction.

Gradually, you will reset your mental programming so that your 'boot up' is not from the false identity of a body, but the higher reality of spirit, from where you will get much greater clarity on every aspect of your life. You could say it is like getting an 'upgrade' to a superior 'operating system' that is generations more advanced than what you had been using. Life will become much more magical, interesting and meaningful. The world around you will seem more colorful, vibrant and easier to navigate. Trust me on this, because like many others before me, I have experienced the incredible benefits of this 'software upgrade.'

You will never again revert to your outdated operating system. It will be forever deleted from your internal 'hard drive.'

However, be warned: although you will experience a higher taste once you reboot your consciousness, there will inevitably be 'viruses' roaming your virtual world ready to infect your consciousness and slow down your new operating system. In this case, run diagnostics by reviewing what you may have done in the recent past to allow such influences to enter your consciousness. Diagnosis is the function of your intelligence, so keep it sharp by regularly reading soul-affirming literature and associating with people who reinforce your core values, not challenge them.

My hope is that the lessons and realizations I will share in this book will inspire you for a lifetime and empower you to handle any challenge life throws at you. Remember: As a soul, you are immutable, unchanging, eternal, all powerful, pure, and blessed.

YANTRA MEDITATION

The use of yantras as tools for meditation, mind reprogramming, or psychic protection, dates back some thousands of years in India. But what exactly is a yantra?

A yantra is a machine or device that delivers a subconscious command to the mind or that carries the vibrational equivalent of a deity or prayer in two- and three-dimensional geometric forms.

I have created a specific yantra for each affirmation and meditation that I will share in this book. Essentially these yantras capture the meaning of each affirmation in geometry. They have been mapped to a very powerful and harmonious magic square of the Sun, wherein all the numbers are arranged so that not only is each one of them mathematically harmonious to all the others, and each row a sum of the Sun's power number of 111, but the sequential placement of each number also creates the most beautiful geometric pattern.

Yantras, talismans and sigils are traditionally created from magic squares, and I have used what I believe is the most powerful of all magic squares to create these special yantras.

I firmly believe they will serve to embed the affirmation deep into your subconscious mind if you take the time to meditate on them while reciting the affirmations.

I AM POWERFUL

Strength

It is imperative that you understand the power that is within you. I am not talking about your physical strength or even your mental powers, but rather the essence of your being—you as spirit soul. This thing we call 'soul' is beyond the perception of the mundane senses or the tools of molecular science, but can be understood by symptom of consciousness.

This soul power that is within you is beyond measure and is the very essence of your existence. The inherent thirst to survive is at the very root of that power and is symptomatic of the soul's immutable nature. Take, for example, the humble blade of grass; it is able to crack the cement pavement, not because of physical strength, but due to the internal urging of a soul to reach sunlight. The same can be said of water; it always seeks the deepest point. It may take thousands of years, but over time, its constant weathering will crack the rock allowing the water to seek the deepest level. Even among martial artists, that fighter who can best align with their *core* is the one that is praised for having the greatest will to win.

When you learn to tap into the unlimited storehouse of soul power, you unleash the potential to make the impossible possible and firmly establish your mark on the world.

Never underestimate the power of soul—for doing so is the greatest injustice to who you really are. So don't sell your*self* short, but honor your inherent power and realize your full potential. Celebrate this truth by honoring every molecule of your being until all you feel is pure joy all the time! You are greater than you can possibly imagine. Inside, at your deepest level of consciousness, surges a hurricane of immense power—spinning with unlimited courage and strength, just waiting to be unleashed. The choice to unleash that hurricane-like power is in *your* hands. If a small plant can break through a mountain rock, you too can break through 'mountains' of obstacles before you. Believe it. You have the strength.

Potential (kinetic energy)

The power of the soul is there within all. It is the common birthright of every living being. Indeed, despite our obvious physical differences, in terms of energetic quality we are all equal to each other and therefore possess the same innate potential. In the same way that a drop of the ocean possesses the same qualities as every other drop and the ocean as a whole, we as spirit are equal in quality to the entire energetic ocean.

For instance, if we could freeze time just before the so-called Big Bang, we would see that, for an instant, only one common energy existed. Everything in the universe emanated from that singular energetic event. Whether we accept that in the beginning the universe was created by a great cataclysm, or by the seed of a pure sound, as in the holy name of God, it makes no difference because ultimately in both scenarios, *energy* is the clear impetus. Every tangible thing we experience in this universe, whether it be mountains, trees, insects, fish, animals, humans, planets, or galaxies, are in essence different forms of the same stuff that stars are made of. Therefore, we have the same energetic potential as everything else in the universe.

We are Little Gods

The corporations that govern this world have sold you a lie. They have told you that you are not good enough; not attractive enough; not strong enough; not smart enough; or not rich enough. All lies, because they are based on a false paradigm, which, sadly, we have all been buying into. That is: We are nothing but a physical body. *No! You are a beautiful, powerful, intelligent, and abundant spiritual being just bursting with loving potential.*

Sanskrit scholar, Srila Prabhupada explains: "… any living entity, being part and parcel of Krishna, has the qualities of Krishna, but just not in quantity." In other words, we are like "sparks to the fire." We are not the fire (or the source of those sparks), but rather are made of the same fire-like (spiritual) energy.

The barrier to our full realization of this potential lies in our ability to manage our mind and deal with our karma. Let me explain …

Managing our Mind and our Karma

To manage the mind means to bring it under the control of the intelligence. You do this by understanding the difference between the two. Essentially the mind conjures up ideas and desires, and the intelligence analyses and decides whether to accept or reject these concepts. Above the intelligence, however, is the soul—the ultimate controller of the body/mind complex—the *witness*, if you will. Unfortunately, due to ignorance of our higher spiritual nature, as a witness to these psychological affairs, we either allow the whimsical mind to dictate the direction of our lives, or we fail to keep our intelligence alert and thus lose all sense of discrimination. India's famous spiritual classic, the *Bhagavad-gita* (Song of God) explains:

> *While contemplating the objects of the senses, a person develops attachment for them, and from such attachment lust develops, and from lust anger arises. From anger, complete delusion arises, and from delusion bewilderment of memory. When memory is bewildered, intelligence is lost, and when intelligence is lost one falls down again into the material pool. (Bhagavad-gita 2.63-63)*

The other component of our potential is karma. Simply put, karma means work, or rather the reactions to the work you have performed. The Bible states: *"As you sow, so shall you reap."* The universe operates on a complex system of give and take in an effort to create harmony. Everything in the universe is seeking balance, or the most natural state of being. It is the same with our karma. As a universal law, karma is always seeking a fair balance of good and evil. If you act in such a way to cause suffering to another, eventually that same suffering will reflect back to you. Not necessarily in this life, but eventually it will catch you, much the same as an old parking ticket may follow you from state to state until you pay it off. Of course, this analogy is overly simplified because karma is an enormously complex web of interactions stretching over vast regions of space and time.

In any case, although our potential is unlimited, it is directly affected by the state of our mind and the 'playbook' of our karma, which subsequently determines the type of physical body we get, the place we are born, and the people we will come into contact with.

Therefore, you have to think carefully about the decisions you make today because they're painting a picture of your future. What you are today is an accumulation of all the decisions and actions you have made in the past. You are entirely responsible for your present situation.

The *Bhagavad-gita* warns us:

The living entity, thus taking another gross body, obtains a certain type of ear, eye, tongue, nose and sense of touch, which are grouped about the mind. He thus enjoys a particular set of sense objects. (15.9)

"No, it is not my fault," you protest. But yes it is, for karma follows us throughout our spiritual evolution and not just in this one lifetime. What is happening today may just as likely be a result of something we did in a past life. The good news is that you do not have to be locked into a karmic downward spiral. If you have learned your karmic lesson, *you can* move on and break the pattern.

You, as soul, the 'witness' *always has a choice* to effect a positive change in your circumstances. Change has to begin *now* though. Not tomorrow, but now! You have to focus all your attention on what is happening around you now, because life really is just a string of 'now' moments. The past is gone forever and will only remain as fragmented pictures in our mind, while the future is always in a state of elusiveness—you can never touch it. All that really matters is *now*. Just as the micro is equal to the macro, or the ocean drop is equal to the quality of the entire ocean, the full power of the cosmic creation is within you. Draw on that source power now and start living life the way *you* want to *now*. And as for past bad karma, well, all you can do about that is to do the right thing *now* and allow whatever lesson is meant to come your way unfold as it is supposed to. Acting in the present is how you live eternally.

Aligning with your Core

To align with your core means to be aware of your inner divinity at every moment of the day. This includes while eating, sleeping, having sex, socializing, defending yourself or when engaged in recreation. If you are conscious of your nature as a soul, your actions and influence on others will powerfully reflect this. Eastern mystics believe that the state of mind of another person can never negatively affect someone who is fully conscious of the presence of God within their heart. This is how the great sages and saints of yore and even in modern times are able to move among us. Christians speak of striving to be "in this world, but not of this world," while Jesus prayed: "They are not of the world, even as I am not of it."[1]

The expression '*Namaste*' when greeting someone in India is to say: "I honor the presence of God in your heart." Acknowledging someone's divinity is the highest honor you can give. The gesture states very clearly that you are not concerned with race, religion, gender, or social status. It is completely non-discriminating. However, we sometimes see people using this expression while privately holding onto feelings of separateness and inequality. It seems that people adopt these foreign expressions in an attempt to feign spirituality, when it would be more sincere to simply express the meaning of *Namaste* through actions of unconditional service.

---

[1] John 17 (New International Version, 2010)

Practical Namaste

There are six ways that unconditional love is expressed in this world between two people. These are:

1. **Revealing our most intimate secrets.** By doing this we align our consciousness with our higher self, our most intimate identity, which is deeper and more subtle than the illusory ego associated with the body.
2. **Hearing in confidence and with an empathic heart.** This requires us to suspend all judgment and honor the true essence of another by embracing their spirit with unconditional love.
3. **Giving a gift for no other reason than gratitude.** Practicing this habit will enrich your consciousness with an "abundance mentality."
4. **Receiving a gift gracefully**. Honoring the giver by gracefully receiving will allow them to foster their unconditional love and service and will help them to realize that there is more joy in giving than in receiving.
5. **Giving blessed food with the pure intention to please.** Since food is the most basic principle of life and the center of every culture, it has a unique role to play in creating peace and unity in the world. When we give pure food with love it creates deep, lasting impressions.
6. **Accepting food that has been given with love**. Just as in receiving a gift, to receive food gracefully is essential for closing the cycle of reciprocation. However, because food is so intimate, it has even more power to heal the soul.

Each one of these acts of unconditional loving exchange enriches the heart of both the giver and the receiver and is therefore the most practical way to express the meaning of *Namaste*.

Purest Love

A person who is truly conscious of their own spiritual nature and the divinity within all other living beings, will naturally filter every experience through that paradigm, and, in so doing, increase their vibration to the point where they consistently attract people and experiences that resonate with that vibration. You'll know when you meet such saintly people because their presence will be overwhelmingly comforting to the point where your heart chakra blossoms and you become like putty—excited and ready to conform to their every wish.

A similar experience can be had when a man and a woman connect in body, mind, and spirit. The love can be so intensely synchronized that each are willing to fully surrender to the other's satisfaction. Unfortunately, such loving exchanges tend to be short-lived because of the nature of conditional desire—it burns high, but does not last forever.

Love in the spiritual realm, however, burns eternally, as perfected in the pastimes of Radha and Krishna. They are one in love, each seeking newer heights of selfless service to the other. It is this ongoing selfless loving exchange that is wanting in the material world. Even the most pure of loving exchanges in this world are temporary and, in one way or another, are conditional.

Srila Prabhupada comments on the pure love of Radha Krishna:

The loving affairs between Krishna and the gopis in Vrindavana are also transcendental. They appear as ordinary lusty affairs of this material world, but there is a gulf of difference. In the material world there may be the temporary awakening of lust, but it disappears after so-called satisfaction. In the spiritual world the love between the gopis (village maidens) and Krishna is constantly increasing. That is the difference between transcendental love and material lust. The lust, or so-called love, arising out of this body is as temporary as the body itself, but the love arising from the eternal soul in the spiritual world is on the spiritual platform, and that love is also eternal.[2]

The Soul is Unborn and Undying

For the soul there is never birth or death. Nor, having once been, does he ever cease to be. He is unborn, eternal, ever-existing, undying and primeval. He is not slain when the body is slain. (Bhagavad-gita 2.20)

Nothing can kill the soul. In fact, according to the Gita, the soul, being transcendental to time, was never born and will never cease to be. You and I are eternal beings and that is why death feels so unnatural and why we have such a difficult time accepting it. The fact is: you never die, but rather, you, the soul that currently animates this physical body, live on forever. Our destination after the death of the material body is determined by your *karma* and desire.

How you act and the thoughts you accumulate in this life are gradually shaping your next body. Notice I did not say 'incarnation' because the fact is that we may not incarnate, or 're-flesh' into another physical body, but move on to a higher plane of consciousness where there is no need for a gross physical body. It all depends on our state of consciousness at the time of death. If your consciousness is fixed on this physical plane, you can expect to remain bound here and take on another physical form. However, if you are able to remain detached from the body by fixing your awareness on your divine nature, you can expect to attain a more subtle form, the highest of which is our original spiritual form, and thus return back to our source, the Godhead.

We can assume, however, that because of our attachments to this physical plane and our need for further enlightenment, most of us will likely have to take another

---

[2] *Teachings of Lord Chaitanya*, Chapter 31.

physical form after this body becomes uninhabitable. And, therefore, the type of body we get will be determined by our karma and impassioned desire.

According to the *Bhagavad-gita,* there are basically three layers to our existence in this world: a gross physical form made up of the five most basic elements (earth, water, fire, air, and ether); a subtle form consisting of mind, intelligence and false ego; and finally a spiritual form from which consciousness evolves and that is the most subtle form of all.

Since the spiritual form is our core, we are addressing the two outer shells. Some esoteric books speak of a combined mind and intelligence as the source of the soul. However, it is important that we distinguish the astral form of mind and intelligence from the even more subtle form of the soul. There is a major difference. Whereas the soul is the driving force behind our very existence, the astral or 'spirit' body is merely the subtle container that carries us to our next destination after the demise of the physical body. The physical body of earth, water, fire, air and ether, or more grossly, blood, muscle, bones, skin, hair, pus, bile, mucus, and so on, provides a medium for the soul to express itself in this physical plane. Its existence is temporary and over time it goes through dramatic changes, finally returning to its most basic constitution of the five gross elements. The astral body, on the other hand, lives on past so-called 'death,' carrying the soul (consciousness) to its next destination. Depending on the condition of the astral body, the soul will either reincarnate into a lower or higher birth in this physical world, or move beyond the limitations of the five gross elements by resonating at a higher frequency of consciousness. In other words, the more conscious you are of your higher *self*, the higher or more pure your destination will be. However, in using the word 'destination,' I am not implying some distant place out in the galaxy.

Theosophist and clairvoyant Charles Leadbeater described it this way:

"... the sub-planes (subtle realms) must never be thought of as divided from one another in space, but rather as interpenetrating one another; so that when we

say that a person passes from one subdivision to another, we do not mean that he moves in space at all, but simply that the focus of his consciousness shifts from the outer shell to the one next within it."

The ultimate destination of every soul is to return back to the energetic Source, the Godhead, the highest and subtlest of all planes of consciousness. To achieve success will require complete sanitization of the mind and intelligence so that your consciousness is vibrating at such a high frequency that no gross material element can settle. At this stage, the soul sheds all gross and subtle material bodies and realizes its full conscious existence, fully awakening the original spiritual body, spiritual mind and spiritual intelligence.

It is for this reason that all spiritual traditions recommend renunciation of the vices of this world, for by maintaining an attachment for physical things and experiences we attune our consciousness to the frequency of this physical domain. Hence, at the time of death, we will be forced to 're-flesh' to continue experiencing the same things and the mundane show goes on. Sometimes, though, spiritual practitioners misunderstand the full meaning of renunciation, leading them to artificially renounce the world. This is also a trap. Let me explain …

Detachment

We incarnate into this physical world, naked and bereft of any possessions. Whatever we accumulate during our lifetime may be temporarily in our care, but once we give up the physical body, those same possessions are either gifted in the form of a will or distributed by the state. Since we are not able to take anything tangible with us after 'death,' how can we honestly claim ownership? And who is the true owner anyway? According to the *Vedas*, everything that is animate and inanimate in this world is ultimately controlled and belongs to God.

"Out of fear of the Supreme Personality of Godhead, the directing demigods in charge of the modes of material nature carry out the functions of creation,

maintenance and destruction; everything animate and inanimate within this material world is under their control.[3]"

Therefore, to truly renounce something is to not artificially give it away, but rather to fully understand to Whom it belongs to and use it accordingly. In other words, a spiritualist may be living in a great city like New York, but rather than artificially renouncing the comforts of an apartment, they can accept that shelter with the understanding that it is a gift of the Creator and should therefore be used in the service of God in order to bring balance, peace, and harmony to their life. How they do this is a very personal thing, but the foundations of their decision is an acknowledgment that God is the Supreme Controller, the Supreme Owner and the Greatest Benefactor. According to the *Bhagavad-gita*, this is the purest form of renunciation and the ultimate peace formula.

> *"The wise, knowing Me as the ultimate purpose of all sacrifices and austerities, the Supreme Lord of all planets and demigods and the benefactor and well-wisher of all living entities, attain peace from the pangs of material miseries.*[4]"

Learning detachment from this physical world is one of the great lessons we all must contend with. Death is no doubt the most brutal messenger of this lesson, and so we would be wise to prepare for death or the loss of a loved one by cultivating detachment. I am not suggesting you develop a cold and heartless attitude towards the world, but rather the kind of detachment I'm suggesting must be imbued with love within the context of the absolute spiritual reality that you are not this body, but are an eternal spiritual being. So to let go of any attachment to a body is healthy for the soul, and can be a joyful experience when done with the understanding that the departing soul is now free. Death need not be a time of sadness, but can become a celebratory experience as you focus your attention on the soul's success in moving

---

[3] *Bhagavata Purana* 3.29.44.

[4] *Bhagavad-gita* 5.29.

beyond the limitations of a gross body. Granted, even with having this higher understanding, you may still have feelings of grief as you long for the association of that person. However, since the soul is unlimited, there is no reason why a soul connection cannot go on beyond death.

One way to deal with the sadness of loss is to focus exclusively on the positive contributions that person made in your life.

Dealing with Attachment

Being absorbed in matter prevents a materialistic person from understanding their higher *self*. Although an intellectual or philosopher may be able to discriminate between matter and spirit, it does not mean they'll be able to transcend attachment to matter. However, a yogi, the best of whom are the bhakti-yogis, being exclusively fixed on the ideal of transcendence from matter, can easily attain ultimate success.

In other words, the materialist is completely in illusion; the philosopher may not be in complete illusion, but neither do they possess absolute knowledge; but the bhakti-yogi is completely on the spiritual platform, as Krishna confirms in the *Bhagavad-gītā* (14.26):

> *One who engages in full devotional service, who does not fall down under any circumstance, at once transcends the modes of material nature and thus comes to the level of Brahman.*

A yogi with devotion is therefore in the most secure position, having reached a state of transcendental consciousness, even while conducting themselves in material affairs. While philosophers and haṭha-yogis can only gradually ascend to transcendental consciousness by nullifying their material discrimination on the platform of psychology and nullifying the false ego, by which one thinks, "I am this body, a product of matter."

Srila Prabhupada comments, "One must merge the false ego into the total material energy and merge the total material energy into the Supreme Energetic. This is the process of becoming free from material attraction."

Srila Prabhupada suggests here that by engaging all energies in the service of the energetic Source, one is able to achieve liberation from mundane attachment.

YANTRA & MEDITATION

I AM POWERFUL

I am a soul with unlimited potential.

I am aligned with my core essence.

I am eternal and transcendental to this material energy.

I AM POWERFUL

I AM PROTECTED

Sense of Security

Every living being in this world is part and parcel of the Supreme. We are essentially all part of a universal family of life. If we are to accept the modern belief that at one point in time there was a Big Bang that created all material matter, then it follows that each and every one of us is historically related to that single point of energy before the so-called Big Bang. No exception. What this means in a spiritual sense is that we all have the same source or same Godhead from which we emanated from. You may call that Source one name and I call it something else, but arguing over the name of God is a moot point, because ultimately, by definition, there can only be *one* Source or *one* Godhead—and this Source is the same for all of us.

In the Christian patriarchal traditions, God is referred to as the Father. In pagan traditions, God is referred to as the Mother Goddess, and in others the Great Spirit. In each one of them, it is accepted that the Supreme is not only a great benefactor of mankind, but our protector as well. Just the same as when a child sleeps in her mother's arms, the soul 'sleeps' in the 'lap' of this physical world, dreaming various incarnations into play, while the loving eyes of the Lord look on.

The *Bhagavad-gita* describes the soul (*atma*) as a bird sitting in a tree (the body) and sitting beside that bird is another bird known as the *Paramatma* (supreme soul), who is witnessing the activities of the bird and patiently waiting for it to turn around. The *Paramatma* is the same as what the Christians describe as the "Lord in the heart." There has never been a time when the Lord turned away from us. On the contrary, it is we who have chosen to turn our back on the Lord—the illuminating Sun within and it is this turning away that has created the shadow of illusion and feelings of separateness.

You have to believe, therefore, that no matter what situation you may find yourself in, the supreme soul within is always there and therefore *you are protected*. Ultimately, nothing can kill the soul and the Lord within is always there to help us.

Peace of Mind

The natural peace that a child has while laying in the arms of their mother is something that cannot be artificially created. A crying child will continue to cry until she reaches the arms of her mother. Instinctively the child knows when Mother is there. In the same way, as we develop the confidence and realization that we are never separated from God, it will translate into a sense of peace and contentment that will consume every aspect of our lives. People that come into contact with us will feel that peace and the effect will multiply as that same feeling is reflected back. You may have experienced this when coming into the presence of a great spiritual leader. At that moment, your false sense of identity is suspended, as you bathe in the radiance of that calming vibration. That same peace is obtainable by anyone who is willing to align their consciousness with the vibration of the soul and do what is necessary to rise above the whimsical demands of the mind and the urges of the body.

Peace of mind comes from purity of the heart. The more we align ourselves with the child-like innocence and purity of the soul, the more we will rid ourselves of anxiety, fear, and insecurity.

What does this mean in a practical sense? It means embracing the innocence of childhood; to once again believe in miracles; to expect the best; to be free from fear; and full of hope. Fear is the greatest enemy in this world, and we see that it attacks the very core of our optimistic 'child-like' self. The light of purity is the only thing that can completely rid the mind of fear and negativity. Purity is both a state of mind and an outward expression of unconditional service. Ask the question: Is my motivation pure? Is my mind free of fear? If not, change the programming.

Interdependence

Like a great web of interconnectedness, the Universe runs on a symbiotic flow of loving service. Each of us, from the microbe to the great mountains of this world, are all intimately dependent upon each other. We do not live in a vacuum, for life by definition means service. Without service we feel dead. It is for this very reason why so many retirees return to work—it makes them feel connected and important. Service to others is the innate characteristic or *dharma* of the soul, much the same as the quality of sweetness is to sugar. You cannot separate the quality of sweetness from sugar—it defines it.

Throughout your life you have been serving. As a child, you served your parents; as a young adult playing sport, you served your teammates; as a parent, you serve your children; and you serve your boss through work and the government through taxes. And every day of your life you have served the needs of your body. Service is life.

All things, from insects, to plants, aquatics, and the innumerable single cell organisms that exist everywhere are alive with purpose and the engine of life is linkage or service to others. Everything is linked. Every thing serves. Nothing is truly self-sufficient. Just as water and air are inseparable, so too all living things are interdependent. We are all united in life for our survival on Earth. Serving each other is everything.

This recognition of the oneness of all life and the interdependence of all things will serve to strengthen your will and sense of self worth. You are an important piece of the fabric of life. Relish it.

The Synergy of all Things

Synergy is the interaction or cooperation of two or more organizations, substances, or other agents to produce a combined effect greater than the sum of their separate effects. Stephen Covey, author of the best selling *7 Habits of Highly Effective People* says that we should "appreciate the differences." For only by appreciating those differences can we learn to see the empathic harmony that exists in this world. In a very fundamental way, we all appreciate the differences of the opposite sex.

It is the endless seeking of harmony between the *Yin* and *Yang* energies that enables the Universe to prosper and evolve. You are an integral, synergistic, individual part of this divine Universe. Embrace the fact that without you the Universe would never be the same. You are as important to the Universe as breathing is to the body.

And so, as the body naturally reacts to a lack of oxygen by convulsing, the Universe would react violently to the absence of you.

We are, in fact, a microcosm of the macrocosm. The Hermetic tradition explains it this way:

"That which is below corresponds to that which is above, and that which is above corresponds to that which is below, to accomplish the miracle of the One Thing."

The Chaitanya Vaisnavas[5] expound the philosophy of *Achintya-Bheda-Abheda-tattva*, that each soul is simultaneously equal to and yet distinctly unique from the complete whole—an inconceivable one-ness and difference.

The analogy often used in this context is the relationship between the Sun and the sunshine. For example, both the Sun and sunshine are part of the same reality, but there is a vast difference between having rays of the Sun enter your room, and being in close proximity to the Sun globe itself. Qualitatively the Sun and the sunshine are not different, but as quantities they are very different. Similarly, the individual soul is of a similar quality to the Supreme Being, but does not share these

---

[5] Followers of the Vedic scholar and saint, Sri Chaitanya Mahaprabhu, founder of the sankirtana movement and avatar of Lord Krishna.

qualities to an infinite extent. Thus there is a quantifiable difference between individual souls and the omnipotent Supreme Lord. Another example is that of a drop of water from the ocean and the entire ocean itself; there is simultaneously a oneness and difference between the two. So remember this: We are a microcosm of the macrocosm.

This harmonic convergence of the micro with the macro is also expressed beautifully in procreation; each offspring imbibes the psychological and physical traits of their parents.

We are Never Alone ... Just Forgetful

One of the things that you must keep reminding yourself is that *you are never alone*. It may seem at times that we are so disconnected from the world or that no one understands us or that we are not loved. It happens to all of us from time to time. I can only assume that this is all part of the grand illusion of this world to keep us fearful and bound to this physical frequency, because essentially these concerns are fundamentally body-consciousness.

The more you can remember your true essence as an eternal spiritual being, characterized by the magnificence of godliness in all its variety, to that degree we will escape the delusion of loneliness.

Every day you have to make the effort to refocus your consciousness on the higher frequency of spirit and cleanse the mind of the hankering and lamentations pertaining to the body. The fact is: we are not these bodies. That image looking back at you in the mirror is just a reflection of a temporary shell rotting away and binding you to this dense frequency of matter.

What stops this understanding from becoming fixed in our consciousness is a poorly trained mind that for countless lifetimes has been allowed to recklessly pursue the whims of this grand illusion we call physical life. Matter is just compressed energy and energy is constantly changing shape. Nothing remains the same. All things must change at every moment. There is no such thing as an absolute static state. Life is characterized by motion, in infinite cycles of birth and death.

At some point in time, we all throw our hands up and say, "What is going on here?" "Who am I?" "What is the purpose of my life?" These are all valid questions that have bugged the greatest minds since the beginning of time. And there has never been a shortage of answers to those questions. However, ultimately, *you* are supposed to answer that question. *You* are responsible for your actions and reactions. *You* are the one that determines where you go from here.

It is so easy to just point the finger at God or others as the cause of your mistakes and suffering. However, if we are honest we will admit that we have always had a choice as to how we responded to every situation we found ourselves in. Our God or gods are always there to guide us if we wish, but at no point in time do they interfere with free will. To do so would be contrary to the very nature of love and happiness. Both of which can never be forced. Love and happiness are constitutionally individual subjective experiences unbound by time, place, circumstance and the actions of others. Love and happiness are our true soul nature, and so these two qualities spring from our very core. It is for this reason that humans, not machines, are able to have dynamic, loving, unconditional relationships in the first place.

We are all looking for love and happiness, but unfortunately we look for them in this illusory physical frequency that constantly changes shape. What we need to do is focus this noble pursuit exclusively on the domain from where these qualities emanate from—the frequency of soul. When we start seeing each and every human, animal, insect and plant as a soul expressing itself through a body, we connect with the world at the deepest level. Then and then only can true love and happiness evolve.

The more we do just that, the less we will feel lonely and disconnected and we will begin to, figuratively speaking, bathe in an ocean of connectedness, love and gratitude. It is only then that we can begin to appreciate God's love and our incredible potential as spirit souls. At this stage, life will cease to be a random and chaotic series of rollercoaster rides, but will morph into a divine play where the joy and wonder of life will inspire us at every moment.

YANTRA & MEDITATION

I AM PROTECTED

I now release all fear and anxiety.

Love embraces me every minute of every day, and I am safe from all harm.

I feel totally secure.

I AM PROTECTED

I AM PERFECT

Get in Touch with Your Essence

One thing is absolutely true: there will never be anyone exactly like you. We are all unique individuals. When we were born the mould was broken. So what? Consider this: if one of the reasons that precious gems are so valuable is because of their rarity, then certainly the same must be true of each individual. Of course, what we value is not necessarily the body, but the essence within. When a person dies, we mourn their 'passing,' but where did *they* go to, and who and what is that thing that passed? Obviously, every animate thing in this world is more than the cells that combine to form a body. Our value lays in our essence—the wine within the bottle or the sweetness within the honey. That eternal question: 'Who are we?' follows us from cradle to grave. It is the most primal, gut-wrenching reason to survive. For without striving for that answer everything becomes futile. We need this answer and that is why we live day after day, hoping against hope that the answer will somehow come to us. But alas it eludes us, or does it? Maybe we ignore the answer? Maybe the question has been answered over and over again, but we fail to recognize it? Maybe, if we would just stop asking the question, we might hear the answer.

The answer is simply a reversal of the question: We are who? 'We are' being the operative words and 'who' the qualifier. *We are who* we wish to be. And hence the show goes on. The stage of each life is but the opportunity for each of us to play out a desired persona. The illusion is built into these experiences, for as we don the mask of each persona we add or replace a layer of ignorance over our true *Self*—the essential you within. The eternal 'I' that wills these various incarnations. The real *Self* dreams these fake personas into action. Without the real *Self*, there would be no stage play. This is both sad and encouraging. Sad, because we have wasted so much time play acting, but encouraging because 'we are' and therefore there is some sense of control and free choice at play. The question, therefore, is not 'who are we?' but first, how do I stop taking another material body? If we answer that question, all other questions, including 'Who are we?' will naturally be answered.

The example is given of a drowning man. While being offered rescue he does not bother to ask why or how he found himself in that predicament; he just allows the rescuers to do their job and save him. Once he is safely on dry land, then if he so chooses, he can question the reasons behind his misfortune. More than likely, however, he won't care, for he will be content in his new-found freedom. A wise man does not ponder the struggles of the past, but focuses fully on the good fortunes of the present.

To get in touch with your essence simply means to wake up, stop play acting, and start making conscious choices that will lead you out of the wretched entanglement of another physical body.

Love thy Self

Just as charity begins at home, love must also begin with loving your *Self*. If we cannot love our *Self*, how can we possibly love someone else with all sincerity? To love your *Self* is to love God and all of creation. You are perfect in every way. The apparent blemishes, bumps, and asymmetrical characteristics of your body are as they should be. 'Your' being the operative word, for *you* are not this body, and neither is the body *you*. It is merely our chosen mask for this one lifetime. We had a role in choosing this persona, for it is meant to teach us an important lesson in our quest for spiritual purity. Ironically, the apparent imperfections could be the most effective way to teach us unconditional love.

When you look into the mirror, just remember that the real *you* is looking from behind those eyes. The reflected image of the body you see is merely your vehicle for this one lifetime. It is not your eternal carriage, and neither does it in any way disqualify you or hinder your full potential. In fact, the more imperfect the body is, the more of a blessing in disguise it is. Or should I say, a disguise of a blessing. The blessing being the fact that the real *you* is eternal and never defined by any temporary dress. Know your body for what it is: a carriage for the soul. Love it for what it is, just as you would love an old bicycle. Focus on the good it has done for you and love it. If you can do this with a heart filled with sincerity, surely that love will radiate around you and impact everyone you come in contact with.

We have all had the experience of meeting someone that may not have the body to win a beauty contest, but who radiates with such a high sense of worth and courage that is infectious. We say they have charisma and wonder why we don't have the same. But alas, you do, if only you would stop focusing on your so-called physical limitations and imperfections, and give attention to your core essence—the soul within.

A person that has charisma has tapped into this power source, even if unconsciously, or should I say, without full understanding of the subtleties of soul. They may have just come to realize that they are more than meets the eye, or that they feel bigger than their shoes, mightier than the wind or taller than their small frame. Even if they are not self-realized, they have at least, by good fortune or grace, stumbled upon the seed of the truth—that we are great and the real truth of our being is how we define it, not what others assume to be true.

You are One of a Kind

We are told to conform and be like everyone else and just fit in. The underlying agenda here is simple: the more you behave like a sheep, the easier it is for others to control you and manipulate your mind into doing exactly what the power masters desire. Those that stand up and speak out are punished, ridiculed, and sometimes killed. There is nothing wrong with expressing your uniqueness, because that is essentially the source of our perfection. No two people are the same. So muster the courage to always express your true feelings. Give up the weakness of political correctness and enter the zone of the 'truth warrior'—a frame of mind where your soul speaks freely and your individuality dances to the rhythm of life, and not the sad song of a stone-faced crowd. Everything about you is unique and beautiful, just the way the Creator wanted it. You are one of a kind, so live your truth now.

Acceptance

Acceptance is the action of consenting to receive or undertake something offered. At every moment we are being offered the unconditional blessings of the Universe; however, we often fail to recognize those blessings, and instead focus on what we don't have. According to the great *Law of Attraction*, one of the essential ingredients for attracting what we want is to first appreciate all of which we have now. By embracing the good in our life with open arms of gratitude, we emit a vibration that must by definition attract more of the same—for like attracts like.

Learning to accept, however, does not mean agreeing to a sub-standard life, or circumstances that are not to your liking. You must always believe in your greatness and desire accordingly. Learning to accept, therefore, must always be within the context of your innate greatness. You need to accept the blessings that surround you and keep your heart open for more of the same.

Do not be Distracted by External Illusions

Although in the most pure sense of the word we are perfect in every way, it is human nature to seek out and be attracted to all forms of perfection. We desire and hanker for things we don't have, because in some way we perceive those things to be perfect or to possess some quality that we feel is lacking in our own self. This is the great illusion of material life: the grass is always greener on the other side of the fence. Birth after birth we have relentlessly chased the phantasmagorical flamboyance of *Maya* (the illusory material energy) in the hope that by obtaining certain things we will become happier. The truth is that being wealthy does not necessarily equal happiness. In fact, we already possess all that is needed for our absolute happiness. We are not lacking in any way whatsoever. This is true in both the spiritual and material paradigms. In the higher dimension of soul, we are perfect and complete. As Christians are fond of saying, we are "made in the image of God." Similarly, on the material plane, although we may apparently be lacking something, we are always perfectly situated at every moment. The incarnation we have now is a direct result of our past decisions, and therefore the most suitable condition for our current state of consciousness and for the experiences we are meant to have.

We need to be thankful for all that we have now and completely believe that all that we want is already within our possession. Everything in this world begins as a thought. Therefore, we need to solidify these hopeful thoughts of happiness and success by acting as if we are currently enjoying them. This in essence is the science behind the *Law of Attraction*.

The essential point here is to *not* focus on or feed any external illusion that will in some way hinder our progress towards ultimate happiness. If our consciousness is fixed on the reality of our divinity, there is no harm in desiring all kinds of riches, for it is our soul right. There is nothing wrong in wealth. Nor is being rich in some way an obstacle on the path of self-realization. It is not the nature of the thing that is good or bad, but how we use those things. Just the same as a knife can be benefic in the hands of a trained surgeon and yet malefic in the hands of a criminal.

Do not therefore be distracted by negative thoughts of failure, or foolish notions that failure or poverty is your lot in life. God wants us all to be successful. Such distracting illusions do not necessarily only mean things of debauchery. Thoughts of mediocrity are just as illusory, for the soul by nature is far from mediocre. We are perfect in every way and therefore deserve only the best the Universe has to offer.

When you feel overwhelmed by negative thoughts, it is a sign to recalibrate—to reset your internal programming. Just the same as restarting your computer or clearing the cache and whatever 'bugs' may be causing issues, we sometimes need to do the same with our brain and mind.

A practical suggestion would be to take the time to focus exclusively on what is great about your current situation. If necessary, compile a list. Express your appreciation for what is good by keeping a journal or talking to friends. For example, let them know how much you appreciate their presence in your life.

The more you can focus on what is right, the less chance your mind will wonder into the caverns of despair and negativity. But if it does, bring it back immediately. Remember, you are not your mind. You are spirit—the 'witness' and therefore always have the final say.

YANTRA & MEDITATION

I AM PERFECT

I embrace my perfection and the core essence of my being.

I love myself unconditionally.

I accept everything about my life as truth.

I AM PERFECT

I AM PRASADAM

Mercy

The Hindu concept of *prasadam*[6] is synonymous with grace or mercy—or that which is unconditionally manifest by divine providence. By definition, therefore, we too must be *prasadam*, for our very manifestation was an act of unconditional love. Have you ever paused to think of why you exist in the first place? We often frustrate ourselves over the eternal question of what is the purpose of life? But more importantly, we should be asking, "Why do I exist in the first place?"

According to the Vedic scriptures, the soul is a microcosm of the Personality of Godhead—qualitatively equal in all respects. The word qualitative signifies that we possess all the qualities of divinity—knowledge, eternity, and absolute bliss. The Christian concept of an intolerant Patriarch that smites humanity for their transgressions is not consistent with the absoluteness of divinity. God, by definition, must possess all the qualities that we experience in this world, except to an infinite degree, including masculinity and femininity, personality, humility, tolerance, compassion, forgiveness, happiness, and love.

The pleasure that we experience in loving relationships with our children, spouse, parents, friends must, by absolute definition, also be fully present in God. God is much more than some angry, finger-pointing Patriarch instilling fear in his children. God is everything that denotes a Supreme Personality, including the capability and desire to engage in a variety of loving relationships; to enjoy fun and exciting activities, and do whatever is necessary to expand and heighten such bliss. Each one of us is a direct result of these actions. In other words, we have been created to facilitate the ever-expanding bliss of Godhead, and because we are ourselves a microcosm of the unlimited Godhead, we enjoy as well.

---

[6] Sanctified plant-based food that has been offered in ritual to God or the Goddess.

The question might be raised then, "why is there so much suffering in the world?" To answer this solely from the perspective of matter would make us ignorant of our inner brilliance and perfection as a soul. Just as it would if we were to focus on the masks of the 'stage actors' and their respective parts in the 'play of life,' and ignore the fact that they have a reality beyond the 'stage,' complete with a different name, relationships and passion.

So the real question is, "Who is really suffering?" If we are not these bodies, then are we, the soul, really suffering? In the absolute sense, no, we are not suffering, for the soul is immutable and eternal. However, the essential problem is that we, the soul, are falsely identifying with our physical body and subsequently empathizing with the suffering as well.

By focusing on our inner divinity, however, we align our consciousness with absolute reality and this fixed mindset will lead to a gradual unraveling of the material 'blindfold.' It may take time—possibly many, many births before our awareness fully blossoms, but upon awakening, the so-called births we took will seem no more significant than a dream.

Time itself is an illusory apparition of the material realm. It does not exist in the spiritual plane but is conspicuous only by its absence. The absurd question posed by atheists, "So what was there before God?" fails to take into account that time is a relative participant within this material world and that an absolute God, by definition, must be transcendental to all things relative, including time. In other words, there was never a moment when God did not exist.

"*Time I am, destroyer of the worlds*[7]..." explains Krishna in the *Bhagavad-gita*, alluding to the fact that time eventually destroys all. Nothing is permanent in this material world and this powerful force we call 'time' is under God's control.

---

[7] *Bhagavad-gita* 11.32.

Sadly, our brains are so hardwired to the notion that everything has a beginning and end, that we foolishly place the same time limitations on God.

Interdependence

Another aspect of our '*prasadam*' nature is the fact that everything that we currently possess, and every facet of who we are today, is due at least in part to the mercy of someone else. Your hard work might have opened doors and enabled you to accumulate wealth and knowledge, but ultimately these rewards have come as a result of the cooperation and service of others. There is no exception to this truth, because life is all about linkage. Every living thing is dependent on the life of another. Symbiosis governs nature. We are interdependent beings. Understanding the nature of this interdependence is critical to attaining a peaceful mind.

We came into this world naked and will leave without a single physical possession. Everything we now claim as ours is really just on short-term loan until it becomes the possession of someone else, either through force or surrender.

The more we can accept the temporal nature of this physical world, the easier it will be for us to progress beyond the entrapment of this mortal frame.

Similarly, the more we can appreciate and have gratitude for the service and mercy of others, the greater the sense of peace and contentment will bathe our conscience.

Sympathy and Empathy

Because the constitutional quality of the soul is mercifulness or *prasadam*, it is natural for an enlightened soul to feel the suffering of others and desire to help them. Just as it is natural for us to care and love our immediate family, for the enlightened soul that natural and unconditional affection extends universally, embracing all living things. How is this possible? Because, in truth, every living thing springs from the same energetic source, and therefore all of us resonate with a familial ocean of empathy.

To empathize is to understand and share the feelings of another; however, to sympathize is to agree and practically express your affection. In both cases, you are aligning yourself with the heart of another and taking the time to acknowledge their predicament or value their opinion. Both are important on the path of spiritual evolution, which by definition must espouse tenderness and respect.

Sympathy and empathy are a natural expression of a heart filled with love.

What you give out comes back to you tenfold. The more love you give, the more love will come racing back into your life.

Remember: You are loved, because *you* have the capacity to love someone else.

Selflessness

A mother's love for her child is the most unconditional expression of love in the Universe. For men, it is hard to fathom the depth of the love a mother feels for her child. Indeed, no mountain is too high, no ocean too large, and no predator too ferocious to dampen a mother's unbridled determination to protect her offspring.

Selflessness by definition is best expressed in that maternal relationship. To be honest, a mother's sacrifice, literally and figuratively, has no comparison. A man's attempt to understand is no more effective than a child trying to catch the moon. Men will never understand the pain of childbirth, nor the sacrifice a mother endures to raise a child. However, this is not to say that a male cannot experience selfless love. It is our constitutional nature to love unconditionally, and so for a male, selfless love will tend to manifest in a relationship with a woman—the embodiment of unconditional love in this world when they take the role as a mother.

In essence, for anyone to truly understand selflessness, we can only *try* to learn from the example of a mother. However, somewhat fortuitously, a mother naturally learns how to love unconditionally from the child. It is said in India: "A child gives birth to a mother." And herein lies the beauty of this seemingly unreachable quality—we *all* play a role in teaching each other, for all of us were once children, teaching our mother this most wonderful trait.

Blessing Others

To bless another person is not the exclusive domain of the saints and sages, but is within the capacity of every one of us. To bless someone is to intentionally desire good on their behalf, or to direct the flow of Universal love that embraces all of us towards another person.

The blessing can be in the form of well wishing words, written or spoken, or it can be in the form of thought. Our mental images are the very seeds of manifest form, so when we desire good for another person, we are, in effect, forming that desire in our hearts and projecting it into the Universe.

It is said that the most auspicious thing in the Universe is the association of a saintly person, specifically a genuine devotee of God. The logic behind this is obvious: a genuine devotee of God wishes good for all living beings and rejoices in their happiness. To be in their company, therefore, is like being swept up by a strong current flowing towards the shore of truth and eternity. The so-called 'life struggle' becomes effortless and one can relax and go with the flow of their loving intentions, knowing that they are absolutely certain to reach their desired goal.

Servitude

Serving is the innate quality of the soul, just as sweetness is the innate quality of sugar, or heat is the innate quality of fire; similarly, to serve is a natural expression of the soul. Indeed, it is so natural to us, that even in our most ignorant condition, we still want to serve. Service is life.

A man serves his boss; a mother serves her child; a child serves their teacher; the government serves their constituents; a dog serves its master; a human even serves their pets; and we all serve our body when we eat, sleep, and exercise. Service is the very essence of our existence. We can't escape it, nor do we want to, for service defines us, enriches us, heals our souls, satisfies our minds, and completes all relationships.

Learning to serve with sincerity and love is what separates the genuinely pious from the egocentric.

The key to happiness is to always be expanding and nourishing our service spirit. A practical way to expand and nourish your service spirit is to do one act of unconditional kindness every day. It might be as simple as opening the door for a stranger, making a random donation, feeding a stray animal or baking cookies for your postman. Try it and see how you feel.

The Gopis

In the pastimes of Krishna, the famed speaker of the *Bhagavad-gita* and legendary cowherd boy of Vrindavan, the village maidens, known as the gopis, are considered the embodiment of unconditional loving service. Their example is unprecedented in the history of religious literature. The leader of the gopis is Srimati Radharani, considered the source of the Divine Feminine and the eternal consort of Krishna.

The *Vaishnava* scriptures of India describe that the soul can have one of five loving relationships with God: neutral, servitude, friendly, parental, or conjugal. These statements should not surprise us because whatever is present in this material realm must have a pure source in the spiritual realm, just like the reflection of our image in a mirror.

In the example of the gopis, they rejected all social convention and completely surrendered to the will of Krishna, without consideration for their own reputation or happiness. Their expression of love for Krishna was spotless and devoid of any tinge of mundane lust. Commentators outside the tradition have difficulty separating the gopis' passion for Krishna from the mundane feelings that a young girl feels for a young boy, and therefore they project images of mundane sexuality. However, it must be noted that both Krishna and the young maidens of Vrindavan were no older than 10 years of age, and therefore even from a mundane perspective, they had not as yet developed physiologically to express such physical passion. Their unconditional love for each other was therefore absolutely pure.

YANTRA & MEDITATION

I AM PRASADAM

Everything I am today is due to the mercy of others.

I am open to continue receiving the mercy and love of others.

I offer mercy back to the world through acts of unconditional kindness.

I AM PRASADAM

I AM PROSPEROUS

The Law of Attraction

Thoughts are things that permeate and feed the creation of the world around us. An apparent *Law of Attraction* seems to underlie every single action and reaction in this universe. As you think, you are literally laying down the building blocks of your reality. A person with an 'abundance mentality' has no sense of lack in their heart and thus their consciousness attracts prosperous things to happen to them over and over again. On the other hand, someone who sees only limitation and lack in their life will create barriers in their mind and thereby limit the natural flow of good fortune, and thus they may have to constantly struggle for survival. Such a miserly consciousness closes the heart to the 'sunshine' of good fortune.

The *Law of Attraction* states that whatever you believe with all your heart will be your truth. Or as Henry Ford stated: "If you think you can do a thing or think you can't do a thing, you're right."

You Deserve the Best

The Bible states that man is made in the "image of God." The *Vedas* declare that you, the soul, are qualitatively equal in all respects to God. Naturally, therefore, you and I deserve the very best the Universe has to offer. It may sound precocious to declare such favor when we are obviously so entangled in this material domain; however, the fact remains that the Godhead, as a loving Mother and Father figure, only wants the very best for their children, and therefore we should always expect such favor.

Wallace D. Wattles puts it this way:

"It is perfectly right that you should desire to be rich; if you are a normal man or woman you cannot help doing so. It is perfectly right that you should give your best attention to the Science of Getting Rich, for it is the noblest and most

necessary of all studies. If you neglect this study, you are derelict in your duty to yourself, to God and humanity; for you can render to God and humanity no greater service than to make the most of yourself."

We are all Equal

The *Bhagavad-gita* offers an insight into the nature of spiritual equality:

"The humble sages, by virtue of true knowledge, see with equal vision, a learned and gentle brahmana, a cow, an elephant, a dog and a dog eater (outcaste)[8]."

The purport is that a truly wise person does not make any distinction on the basis of species or social status; they see beyond the external temporary covering of a material body and acknowledge the presence of a life force within. This life force or soul (*atma*), according to the *Bhagavad-gita*, is always accompanied by a *Paramatma* (*Param:* Supreme; *Atma:* Soul) or God in the heart.

If the nature of God is love and compassion, we can naturally conclude that God is equally kind to everyone, because a loving God would treat every living being as a friend regardless of the circumstances of the individual *atma*.

Although the body is made of gross matter, the soul within is of the same spiritual quality as the Supreme Soul. The *Bhagavad-gita* explains that the *Paramatma* or Supreme Soul is an expansion of God within this material world. However, the qualitative similarity of the individual soul and Supreme Soul does not make them equal in quantity, for the individual is present only in one particular body, whereas the *Paramatma* is present in all bodies. The presence of the *atma* and *Paramatma* is what animates all material bodies. A dead body is by definition devoid of the presence of the host soul (*atma*) and Supreme Soul (*Paramatma*).

---

[8] *Bhagavad-gita* 5.18.

A truly learned person is aware of this presence and is therefore respectful and compassionate to all living beings.

The Rain does not Discriminate

The rain falls indiscriminately on mountains, oceans, rivers, and deserts. There is no possible way to know exactly where a particular raindrop will fall. Its inevitable fall to earth is the result of a combination of natural phenomena, the least of which is the mercy of God. The message here is that when mercy descends it is often just like rain—indiscriminate. In other words, you and I are just as worthy as the next person for some unexpected drop of good fortune.

Because we are by nature qualitatively like God, we should expect only the best at every moment. There is no benefit in maintaining a defeatist attitude, because in ultimate reality, you, the soul, can never be harmed, cheated, or exploited. By aligning our consciousness with this higher spiritual truth, we will naturally feel blessed and content, regardless of our present circumstances. This optimistic and blissful vibration will serve to attract all that we sincerely desire.

We are Heirs

If you believe you're a child of God, then you also need to embrace the fact that you are worthy of God's kingdom. Sure, we may feel that we don't deserve such good fortune because of our past inauspicious behavior; nonetheless, by spiritual heritage we are still worthy. But even considering spiritual heritage, why is it that some people are born into wealth while others struggle their entire life just to make ends meet? You may be surprised that the decision is not entirely in the hands of God.

You see, even if a wealthy father bequeaths his entire wealth to his son, if that son is in ignorance of his father's wealth, he may not act appropriately to inherit the good fortune. Such is the predicament of most people today; they are totally unaware of their divine heritage as a child of the Supreme Personality of Godhead—

the source of all opulence, and therefore they do not act in ways that allow wealth to come into their lives. They have convinced themselves that poverty is their lot in life and that nothing ever goes right for them. It is a self-serving prophecy that enslaves them into poverty consciousness. If you've found yourself in this trap, get out *now!* You have the power to do so, and it all starts with reprogramming your mind.

Prosperity Consciousness

The first rule of wealth is to act as if you already have wealth. This means really believing it from the core of your being and behaving accordingly. There are many tactics you can employ to help you establish a prosperity mindset. One trick I have applied in the past is the 'I already have it' game. It goes like this: As you pass by something that catches your fancy, you say to yourself, "I already have it." Similarly, if you are in need of a particular quota of cash to meet an expense, you can repeatedly say to yourself, "I already have (whatever amount of money is needed)." What this exercise serves to do is to put your mind at rest so that you then behave more natural and detached. I have found this technique to be very effective in direct sales when I have had a particular quota to meet for the day. Before going out of the house and throughout the day, I would repeatedly say, "I have already made $1000 (or whatever my quota was)." As I did this, I found my entire demeanor transform so that whomever I then met felt relaxed in my company and did not sense any pressure from me to buy. Rather, they felt I was already successful for the day and believed that so many others had already bought my product, and therefore they should too!

Once you firmly establish a detached and successful mindset, it will translate into a successful body language, tone of voice and sense of contentment, and you'll find helpful people. Prosperity will be drawn to you like a magnet.

Motivational speaker Brian Tracy believes there is a *Law of Expectation*. He states:

> *"This law says that whatever you expect with confidence, positive or negative, becomes your reality. If you confidently expect to succeed, if you confidently expect to learn something from every experience, if you confidently expect to become wealthy as a result of applying your talents and abilities to your opportunities and you maintain that attitude of confident expectations long enough, it will become your reality. It will give you a positive optimistic cheerful attitude that will cause people to want to help you, and will cause things to happen the way you want them to happen."*

Another technique I have used is to always have $100 in my wallet so that whenever I pass by something that I desire in a shop window I can inwardly say, "I can buy that if I want to." This exercise will set your mind at ease, knowing that you have the capacity to get what you want. But for the time being you choose not to act on this power.

Essentially, what is needed here is to reprogram your mind, so that you fully believe that you deserve the best and that, in fact, you already are successful, but that time alone is all that is separating this truth from manifest reality.

Self-satisfaction

One of the keys to happiness is learning to be content with your own company. As long as you believe that satisfaction and love are something that you must find outside of you, you will never be fully satisfied. So the foundation of any prosperity consciousness needs to begin with self-satisfaction and gratitude for what you have now, which begins with appreciating everything about you and taking the time to honor yourself through these positive affirmations.

YANTRA & MEDITATION

I AM PROSPEROUS

I am a child of the Supremely Opulent.

I embrace my godliness and believe that I deserve the best.

I allow myself to receive all good things.

I AM PROSPEROUS

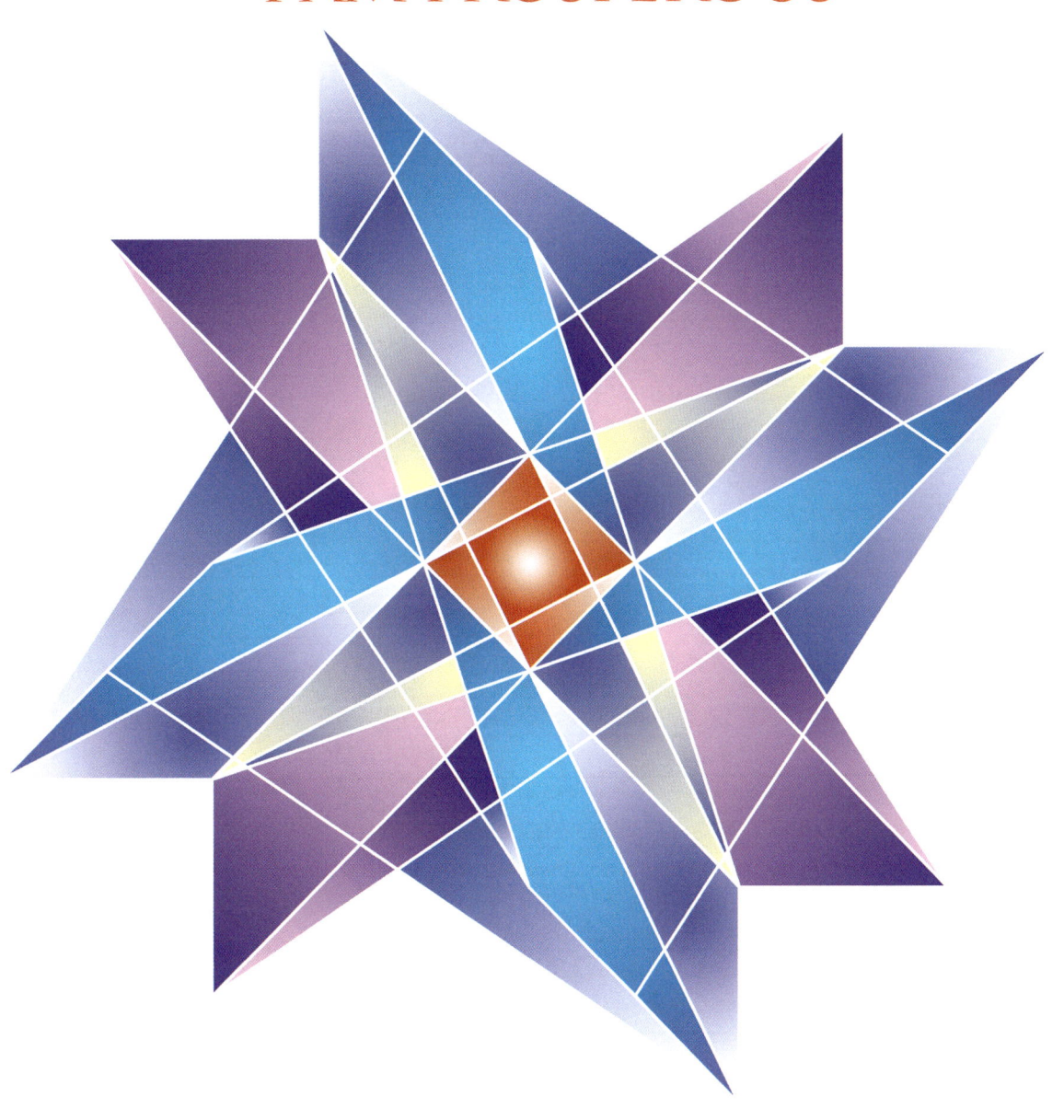

CONCLUDING WORDS

I hope my encouraging words and the affirmations I have provided have brought you to a point of absolute confidence that you are a spirit soul—perfect in every way—protected, powerful, prosperous and constitutionally the personification of mercy (prasadam).

In reading this book you have taken a huge step in resetting your entire life to one of ultimate success, beyond the limitations of this mundane realm and far exceeding any measure of material success. You stand tall as a warrior of truth on top of the highest mountain, where you clearly see the world in all its naked beauty, free of the falsity of ego and temporality.

Nothing can stop you now, if you choose, not even the powerful and flickering mind, so long as you continue to keep your intelligence sharpened by the sword of knowledge and illumined by the association of wise confidants.

I wish you the very best, because I sincerely believe you deserve it. Do you?

WHAT IS A YANTRA?

A yantra is neither magic nor a technique to invoke magic. Rather, in technical terms, a yantra means an instrument, apparatus, talisman, or mystical diagram that encapsulates energetic vibrations. In some Vedic translations, a yantra is described as a machine. Great yogis and ancient writings praised the power of yantras as effective and convenient tools on the path of self-realization. The most famous yantra is the Sri Yantra (below), which is a representation of the divine masculine and divine feminine united as one. It is the Vedic equivalent to the yin yang symbol in Chinese theology.

Symbols and their Hidden Meaning

We express ourselves through the use of symbols, software, and machines all the time. Writing and language are symbolic of our intentions, and in order to express these intentions we often use some apparatus like a pen, or a machine like a computer. For example, consider the symbol for number 7. Factually, it is just two strokes of a pen, but when we see that symbol it reminds us of "lucky seven," seven days of the week, the seven major planets, or maybe something important in our life that happened on the seventh day of the month, etc. In other words, the symbol associated with seven effectively contains a whole databank of information. It is much more than two strokes of a pen.

Aims and Objectives of Yantras

As explained above, we express ourselves through the use of symbols and machines all the time. Yantras also include signs, mantras, and tantra. Different yantras are connected with different deities or angels as well as a specific mantra. The five gross elements of nature, earth, water, fire, air, and ether are also connected to yantras, and by performing specific rituals utilizing the appropriate yantras, it is said that you can control nature.

According to India's ancient Vedic scriptures, a yantra is a science that can be used to connect apparently disparate elements and malefic influences into one harmonizing action. For example, a planet that may normally assert a harmful effect on someone can be countered through the use of yantras. A yantra literally becomes the medium through which the invisible forces of energy can act on an individual.

While anyone could feasibly draw a yantra, it will not yield the desired result unless it is produced with the proper intention and energized with the perfect mantra. Ideally, a yantra should be prepared by a qualified yogi or astrologer, who will prescribe yantras to people to help ward off the evil influence of planets, spirits, or enemies.

Uses of Yantra

Traditionally, a yantra was drawn onto a bronze, copper, lead, silver, stainless steel, or gold plate. However, with the advancement of printing technology, a yantra could feasibly be printed onto a variety of surfaces, depending on the time, place, and circumstance. The medium must first be sanctified by mantra so that the effectiveness of the yantra is increased. Therefore, the yantra's potency is very much dependent upon the purity and sincerity of the person who creates and then energizes it. I spent 14 years of my life as a celibate monk cultivating a pure focused intention, and have studied and the practiced teachings of the most revered spiritual texts in India for almost 30 years.

My Path to Yantras

As a monk, I was introduced to the magic of yantra on my first pilgrimage to India in 1985. At that time, I watched in awe as the pujaris (Hindu priests) performed sacred offering rituals that included the use of some strange geometric patterns. Some of these patterns were inscribed on copper plates and some were even created using colored rice flour carefully arranged at the base of a fire pit surrounded by fruits. The pujari then lit a fire and chanted mantras, pouring ghee to keep the fire blazing as onlookers threw offerings of rice. Drawing a yantra using colored rice flour was the first stage of this elaborate ritual. It was beautiful and mystical, and it never ceased to fascinate my mind.

But why were there specific geometric patterns used and for what purpose? Was it just custom or was their some deeper significance to the geometry? Unlike the tradition of Kolam, where Indian women will decorate the outside of the house with symmetrical patterns drawn with colored rice powder or chalk to invoke prosperity, yantras seemed to contain a mystical power within the actual pattern themselves.

Many years later, during my study of numerology and the magic art of talisman creation and sigils, I learned of the mathematical significance behind yantras and their relationship to magic squares and numerology. A classic example of a magic square is the Chinese *Lo Shu (right)*, wherein the arrangement of the numbers from 1 to 9 is harmoniously arranged so that every column and row add up to 15.

6	1	8
7	5	3
2	9	4

What I discovered is that a yantra is neither magic nor a technique to invoke some magical effect, but is more accurately an apparatus or 'mystical software,' if you will, that fully encapsulates the energetic vibration of an intention or deity.

WHAT IS A SOUL YANTRA?

A Soul Yantra is a unique contribution to the ancient yantra and sigil (talisman) traditions and a new genre of modern art. Like the traditional yantras and talismans, a Soul Yantra is also based on the sciences of numerology, magic squares, geometry, geomancy and astrology. However, in this case the encoded data is not a call to some deity or archangel, but is representative of you and your life purpose.

By using a person's name and time of birth and coloring the resulting geometry according to their astrological influences, the Soul Yantra becomes completely unique. In the same way that numerology can encode a person's character and aptitudes in numbers, the Soul Yantra does so through geometry. Your Soul Yantra literally captures your essence in a harmonic geometric pattern—it is essentially your inner spirit captured in art.

Tamal Krishna Goswami

SoulYantra.com

SoulYantra®

ORDER NOW!
www.SoulYantra.com

NOW ONLY
$**79**.95
Normally $120

ABOUT THE AUTHOR

Paul Rodney Turner was born in Sydney, Australia, and grew up in housing commission accommodation in Sydney's sprawling Western Suburbs. From a very early age, he became interested in astronomy, astrology, numerology, billiards, and graphic design.

At the age of 19, Paul left home to live a reclusive life in Sydney's Blue Mountains. At this time he met Jain 108, a budding artist and sacred geometrician who was fascinated with magic squares. Jain piqued Priya's curiosity with these magic squares.

Shortly after Paul joined an ashram to become a bhakti-yogi, taking a vow of celibacy. For the next 14 years, Paul, now known as Priyavrata das — or Priya for short — by his fellow Vaishnava monks, studied the ancient teachings of the *Vedas* as taught by His Divine Grace A.C. Bhaktivedanta Swami. During this time, Priya furthered his interest in the mystical arts of numerology and sacred geometry.

It is no surprise that Paul's fascination with geometry and numbers later parlayed into his contribution to the world of billiards with the invention of the world's best aim trainer, *The Billiard Aim Trainer* (BAT) in 2006, and later with his book, *The Yoga of Pool* that shows how one can become a champion in billiards and in life.

Paul is currently the International Director of Food for Life, a worldwide network of plant-based food relief organizations. For the past 30 years, he has volunteered for the non-profit, helping to expand its reach all over the world, visiting more than 50 countries throughout Europe, Asia, and the Americas. The non-profit currently serves more than two million meals daily to those in need.

In 1993, Paul wrote the official Food for Life training manual, and in 1996 he wrote, sang and produced the first official FFL music CD called *Prasada Sevaya* (service to holy food).

Paul currently lives on Australia's Gold Coast, where he serves the charity Food for Life Global, teaches Food Yoga, and hones his intuitive skills to better serve his clients with accurate numerology readings and inspired designs. He continues to be a practitioner of Vedic philosophy and metaphysics, as well as a writer of poetry and raw food chef.

Web sites:

www.ffl.org - Food for Life Global

www.foodyogi.org - Food Yoga

www.paulrodneyturner.com - Blog

www.soulyantra.com - Numerology and Personal Yantras

Made in the USA
Charleston, SC
26 January 2015